801016

Thorpe
    The shepherd's year.

The Shepherd's Year

The Shepherd's Year

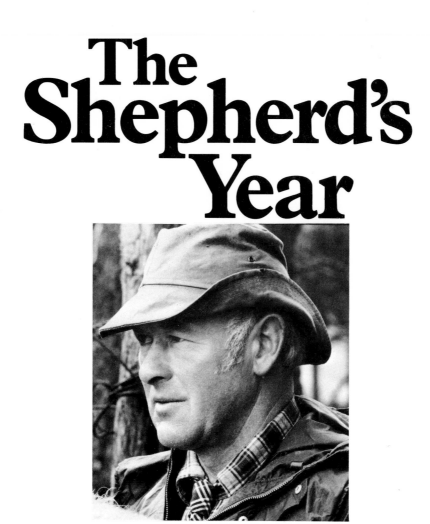

Photographs
DENIS THORPE
Text
ALAN DUNN

David & Charles

Newton Abbot   London   North Pomfret (Vt)

I am grateful to *The Guardian* and the special way they
have of encouraging some ideas, and for their foresight
in letting us follow hill shepherd Ray Dent and his family
through the seasons, making this book about these
marvellous people a possibility.
The photographs are reproduced by kind permission
of the Editor, Peter Preston.

Denis Thorpe

British Library Cataloguing in Publication Data

Thorpe, Denis
  The shepherd's year.
  1. Sheep – England – North Yorkshire – Pictorial
  works 2. Shepherds – England – North Yorkshire
  – Pictorial works
  I. Title II. Dunn, Alan
  636.3′08′3   SF375.5.G7

  ISBN 0–7153–7762–0

Photographs © Denis Thorpe, 1979
Text © Alan Dunn, 1979

Set by Ronset Limited, Darwen, Lancashire
and printed in Great Britain by Biddles Ltd., Guildford
for David & Charles (Publishers) Limited
Brunel House   Newton Abbot   Devon

Published in the United States of America
by David & Charles Inc
North Pomfret   Vermont 05053   USA

The hill shepherd's year is as ordered as the seasons through which it passes, but within the regular beat there is a rich variety of life that is frequently enviable. No two days are alike and the working day and week can often be all one's waking hours. The seasons range from the enclosed white loneliness of snowbound winter to the high heat of summer, when midges by the thousand harass and bite. But the compensations are legion. To be walking, lunch bag at the hip, in the early light of lambing time, with curlew, lapwing and snipe swooping around the twisting burn and sheepdogs brisk and eager, is a form of job satisfaction that few people experience. To help a ewe give birth in soaking rain on the sodden moorland, with not another human being in sight to turn to for help, is to unearth a lean self-reliance and a deep patience. One learns the true values of neighbourliness and a readiness to cushion the occasional rebuffs that nature brings. Not many shepherds would exchange their lot.

The working year begins for all shepherds at mating time, normally much later for the hill flocks than the lowland. By coincidence mating, or tupping as it is universally known, began for Ray Dent's flock of about 2,000 sheep as he and his wife, Lena, walked the hard pavements of London in early December. They were on their way to the Smithfield Show to receive his award as Hill Shepherd of the Year, an annual prize, sponsored by a pharmaceutical firm and a trade journal, since it began in 1973. It was his first visit in two decades, her second, and the pavements were a painful contrast for feet used to the springy turf of the peat-based hills back home in Weardale, on the glorious neck of England.

They felt sorry for Londoners: 'They all seem to have fixed expressions, hurry too much, and talk too quickly.' Ray added

that too many of them looked as though they needed a fluke dose, their eyes dull as those of sheep suffering from liver fluke. The people were kindly, however, and the Dents enjoyed the occasion and had much to tell their son, Ian, when they returned to Glen Whelt farm, its two-feet-thick walls tucked into a hillside 1,300ft above the village of St John's Chapel. They were back just in time, for the Northern Pennines had taken their first heavy fall of snow, making life extra difficult for Ian as he and the dogs gathered ewes off the fells into one of five areas where the rams reigned.

'It's nature in the raw up here at tupping time,' said Ray, as he examined one chastened ram that had moved off its allotted compound and invaded another, only to be repulsed and injured by the reigning rams there. Ray was already aware that he had a problem on hand, for a philandering ram had escaped from the general surveillance of the flock a good month before tupping started. At first it was thought that it had roamed away from the area, or been stolen, but the Dents were later to find that it had mated prematurely with about one hundred ewes. 'He didn't just take a weekend bag with him, he took a suitcase,' Lena drily observed when in the following spring she helped to care for the lambs he had sired.

Tupping is a carefully organised affair for the shepherd. He is aware of the breeding history of his flock, and by coloured marks on the wool, various tags on the ears and careful segregation he guards against the risks of inbreeding. Pride in stocksmanship is all-important, for these are pedigree sheep that Ray looks after, Swaledales, believed to have originated centuries ago in the Tan Hill area at the top end of Swaledale. The breed has special characteristics that enable it to survive at high altitude—up to 2,200ft on the Glen Whelt farm's 3,000 acres—living on coarser herbages, yet so hardy that they can still breed and succour lambs in the worst of weathers and grow a reasonable amount of wool.

Pedigree quality is vital and someone like Ray calls on all his years of experience, and his father's before him, to form a picture of a ram's forebears and their performance before he considers buying during the November sales. Control of the breed is vested in the Swaledale Association, founded in 1920 to build breeding records and assess standards. The major risk is that, for show purposes, the very characteristics that had made the breed pre-eminent could be bred out. Those features in a Swaledale are a good shape, with well-woolled

white flock above four-square black legs, black and white face, with no mix of the hairs, distinctive Roman nose, and a fine sweep of horns.

Once tupping is over in early January the ewes take to the hills and the exhausted rams are moved down to the farmhouse to recuperate. Dependent on the weather there is now a chance for the farmhouse to relax—Ray by painting, with the hills and Swaledale his favourite subjects; Lena at the Women's Institute, or rehearsing a church pageant, or cooking for deep-freezing; and Ian square-dancing in the village hall,

always assuming that the snows haven't cut off the farmhouse.

If the winter is particularly bad Ray prides himself on foreseeing the worst early enough to make certain that the sheep have been moved down to strategic storage points, filled with fodder months previously. Even then heavy snow overnight might trap and bury the ewes, which is when the ever-patient dogs come into their own by sniffing them out. All have the gift, some to an extraordinary degree. In the winter of 1937 Ray had one dog who sniffed out 400 sheep; another, Rock, never lost a sheep in his fourteen years.

Winter is the time, too, when sheep come to the help of birds, by rooting through the crust of ice and snow to reach the grasses and making holes which later the grouse and pheasants enter in search of their rations. This closeness to nature also links father and son when they are out on the fells, miles apart on different hills. By reading instinctively the movement, by season, of grouse, partridge, pheasants, curlews, plover, peewits, redshanks, snipe, mallard and teal they remain aware of each other's position.

With the approach of spring the pace of life at the farm-house quickens, given uncommon emphasis by the early arrival on 21 March of the first lambs sired by the philandering ram—a day marked by snow falling as Ian cleaned the farmhouse chimney and by the resumption of the wet sleety weather known as 'clash' that had preceded the winter snows and given the sheep the worst possible conditions for lambing.

Now the fitness of man and dog is tested to the full. There is no pleasure in rising at sodden dawn, being out on the fells

before first light searching for ewes in difficulty, for lambs in need of mothering. Back for breakfast at 9am, soaked through five or six layers of clothing, hands almost too frozen to wield knife and fork even after vigorous scrubbing. Then back out on the hills, with November's snows still lying under the brow of Swinhope Edge, a chill reminder of one of Ray's worst winters for weather. It would be bad enough for ewes carrying normally, much worse for ewes giving birth a month early.

The switches in diet, lack of vitamin D from the sun, and shortage of minerals from the grasses, especially phosphates, had meant that the ewes had gone into the breeding season not fully equipped for a harsh winter. But for all their personal, wet misery an air of tenderness touches all the Dents' work.

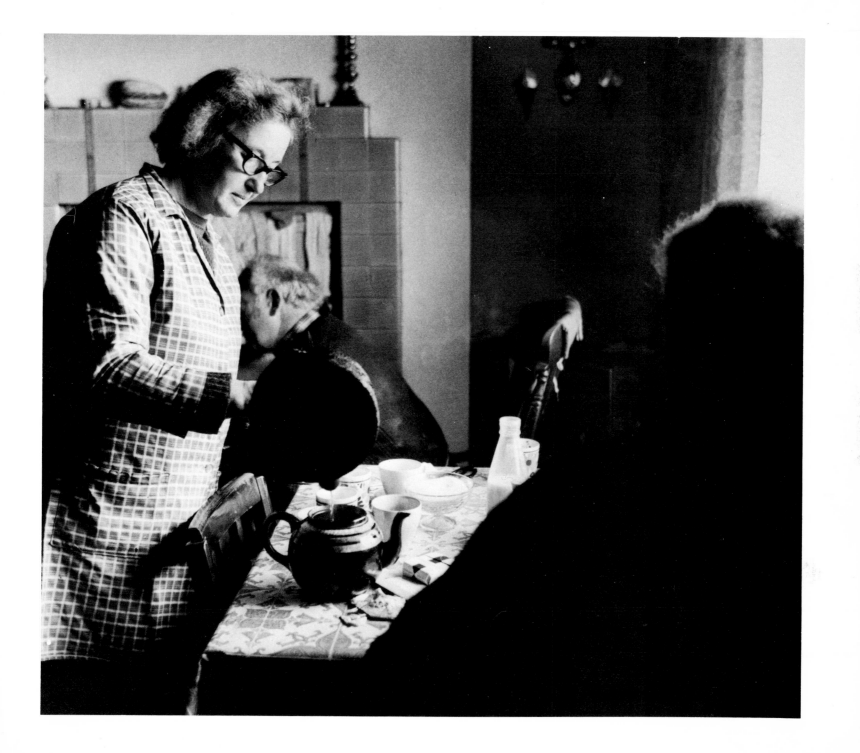

Lambing is the season they like best of all. 'All nature is there,' says Ray, who has a deep regard for nature, 'and you have got to learn to work with nature, not fight her. When you are helping a ewe to give birth to twins you have to sense when she wants help, not tear the lambs out in a hurry to get the job over.' It means, too, keeping walls in good condition for division and shelter, and the dale is glad of the help of a young man who was hiring himself out to repair walls and do other handiwork.

Rural craftsmanship, Ray feels, is vanishing under modern education. No longer do country children learn the arts of self-sufficiency, such as repairing a gate, or growing their own food. Ray and Ian have been shepherds since they left school

and both have been helping at the birth of lambs, calves, kids, pups, kittens and foals since before they went to school. It is still a miracle to them and they still purr over prime-looking lambs, plump and sturdy and lovable on uncertain black legs.

They are familiar with death, too, and try not to allow it to discolour their days when lambs are stillborn. More practically, the skin of the dead lamb is stripped and slipped over a lamb rejected by its mother for some reason so that the mother of the dead lamb will accept the familiar scent and suckle the orphan. There are not many freak births, but Ian, forearms heavily greased, spent a long and anxious time helping one ewe give birth to a dead, eight-legged lamb. 'He saved the mother,' said Ray, proudly and practically.

Now the days are long and absorbing, with regular pacing of the growing flock, trying to anticipate a ewe's difficulties, tramping miles daily at an even pace that sees a man coming home at the same rate as he left it, not like hikers, who take too much out of themselves with a racing start. Swinhope burn, twisting through the lowland, gives them problems, for sheep are always falling in; Ray and Ian will race down the slopes to help them climb up the steep banks. Once a ewe's wool has become soaked in the water the task becomes even harder, but the sheep never learn and the Dents remember sadly one lamb who was rescued three times, only to drown on the fourth occasion.

Lambs and ewes in weak condition are taken back to the farmhouse, where snug dens made from bales of hay in the three barns become temporary nursing homes. In the farmhouse kitchen there is a stirring among some sacking on the hearth of the coal fire, on which a blackened kettle hisses, and a quavery legged lamb, its body still untidily wet, struggles to its feet and pees all over the sacking. 'There's a good chap,' says Lena, for shepherding folk instinctively and perhaps hopefully think of lambs as males.

A lamb born in the wilds has to empty its system early in its life or it risks dying of a chill on the stomach. Lena feeds the lamb a bottle of warm milk from one of the farm's goats, and takes it to its mother in one of the barns, then swings from den to den tending the ailing flock, encouraging a mother to suckle a lamb or feeding by bottle. It is just one of four or five trips she will be making daily to the barns for the next couple of months, in between preparing hot meals from the stock of deep-frozen food: there is no time for ritual cooking when the lambs arrive.

Ray and his son will make three more sorties over the hills with the dogs before bed at 10.30pm, with few days off and only an occasional glance at the television set that has recently entered their lives. More than once the tractor will be run out up the Middleton-in-Teesdale road at night to help a ewe give birth by searchlight under starless skies. Already there are signs that the lambing season will not be good, certainly not matching the previous year's return of 109 per cent. Ray traces the trouble back a year to a long drought, when the sheeps' delicate stomachs grew accustomed to a diet of dry grasses, not even moistened by morning dew. When the drought broke the rains were unceasing for weeks up to the arrival of the snows. The ewes, almost sickened by an unending diet of sodden grasses, were then switched to dry, stored hay. And when the spring did come it was tardy, staying wet and chilly with no encouragement to growth of crops. So the diet swung unhelpfully and mothers and children suffered.

Only slowly did the weather become warmer, but for all Ray Dent's concern for his flock he had time to spare to accompany his boss, John Vicker, on a tour of the fells with a group of conservationists. They were concerned, in a general sense, about the possible ecological risks to a remote and wild area of sheep cropping the grasses. The owners of the farm and Ray sought to convince the conservationists that sensible shepherding found a natural balance in numbers and usage. Many hill shepherds have a deep understanding of the balances generally sought and achieved in agriculture. Ray is sharp to criticise authority in its attitude: 'For too long the demand

has been for change, but it has not all been for the good. Look at the policy of getting rid of hedgerows to create larger crop areas. It may be right on occasion, but has not been generally successful, not least because it affects the general balance with nature.' He points out that as farms have been enlarged and merged, there have been fewer opportunities for young people hoping to build up a farm, which in turn weakens the bargaining position of the National Farmers Union. 'Look at the French. The strength of their farming lies in the number of their small farmers.'

He also questions whether too much theory is being taught at agricultural colleges. 'Young people should get their hands dirty then stir in the theory. At the moment it is theoreticians teaching theoreticians with little practical knowledge among them.'

When the sun eventually comes through undimmed and the breeze is soft, Weardale is an enviable place in which to work and play. Bird song hangs over the high fells and young grouse, pheasant and partridge pick innocently at the fresh grasses among the silent gun-butts on the moorland of

Newbiggin Common, over Swinhope Head on the way to Middleton-in-Teesdale. Curlew, snipe and lapwing wheel over the shimmering Swinhope burn and a distant cuckoo calls. With the heat come the midges, buzzing in thousands around the sweating faces of Ray and Ian as they separate lambs from ewes in drystone-walled pens built in the eighteenth century.

The whole flock is channelled through a narrow passage at the head of which Ian operates a wooden gate to separate mother and child, right and left. Later the same time-honoured method will be used to segregate other categories of age and sex, according to the code of dyed marks on wool or coloured tags on ears.

The flock has been brought down from the fells in two batches, a weakened flock after the poor weather, but generally in good heart. The gather is spectacular. A neighbour helps Ray and Ian and their nine dogs to comb and marshal the sheep on Chapel Fell and then Black Hill. Here is where the dogs can save hours of unnecessary chasing after straying sheep. Fly, a lean, black-and-white bitch with penetratingly alert eyes, is Ian's favourite dog and gives an intelligent sample of her work as Ian explains how just one or two whistles had sent her off. 'She'll make a circuit of perhaps half a mile, a good wide out-run we call it, always keeping out of sight of her target sheep. She can work both sides, but perfers to go left. If she were to go straight for the flock they would be scattered and gone before Fly could get to them. And that would mean more work for Dad and me.' He whistles another dog away to help Fly and moments later the pair were working a group of ewes and lambs down the hillside at a steady, unhurried pace, convincingly in charge.

Separation gives Ray the chance to check his flock thoroughly for the first time since lambing. A lamb born with a withdrawn lower lip was having difficulty in nibbling short grass, and was selected to go to the parent lowland farm, where it might be able to crop longer, richer grasses 'but would never make much'. A ewe had shed her pelt, a sign of shortage of protein, and it had wrapped round her rear legs, cutting them as though scorched by a rope. Sheep with signs of worm are dosed, horns and feet checked, and the larger lambs by the philandering ram are given special marks to enable a later check on the quality of their mothers. If the tup lambs—male—are from sound Swaledale breeding stock, rather than from some of the mixed breeds also kept on the farm, they may later be saved to become breeding rams. If not they will become meat.

For most of the tup lambs, separation means castration. Their fate is known before they are conceived, for the method of putting rams with certain ewes provides the continuity and type. 'It's a regular marriage guidance council we run up here,' says Ray. Castration, by a rubber ring method, is necessary, he explains, or hormones would feed into the flesh and give a

slightly bitter flavour instead of the gamy taste that happens to be popular around Christmas in the Manchester area. Some of the lambs are surprisingly spring-heeled, racing up and along the six-feet-high stone walls like wall-of-death riders in an attempt to join their mothers. Some succeed, but not for long.

The separated ewes and lambs chorus long and plaintively to be reunited—the Glen Whelt chorus, Ray calls it. Happily even sheep have different accents, the thicker-necked lowland breeds uttering the traditional 'baa-baa', while the hill sheep's call is more of a 'mare-mare' with an occasional rolling of the 'r'.

Once castration is over and lambs have been marked for future reference the flock is taken to a larger compound to allow lambs and ewes to 'mother up' before they are again returned to the fells. Four of the experienced dogs—Fly, Jed, Beaut and Spot—work away, defying the tiredness that must be in their bones from the long gather. 'Dogs are like humans,' says Ray as one dog seems to ignore an order, 'they need discipline, but every now and again you have to allow them to use their own initiative.' Unlike the sheep, the dogs never make a sound.

The flock is not left long on the hills for shearing time quickly arrives. Normally this is delayed until a good rise of new wool has started to grow and until it is reasonably warm. Again the flock is gathered, but this time the sheep are taken all the way down to the farmhouse in batches.

Shearing is one aspect of a shepherd's life that has changed totally. Until the arrival of electricity at the farmhouse six years before, shearing was a social occasion, with about a dozen neighbours kneeling in a ring on moorland peat-moss laid on a barn floor, all using hand blade-clippers. They took it in turn at each other's farms. Before the days of freezers it was difficult for Lena to plan catering for them without any certainty that numbers would be right. But it was always cheerful.

Now Ray and Ian work alone with electric clippers and an easy, practised rhythm that sheds the wool from the sheep in one piece in moments. World records—fifteen clipped in nineteen minutes in Australia—mean nothing to Ray, for the clip allows the pair to make another check on the health of the flock and perhaps trim horns and feet and give doses. 'But I was once timed at two in three minutes with hand shears,' he admits. 'I was quite fast then.' Electric shearing was not all that faster, he felt, and in some senses was more tiring; working

with the sheep upside-down between his feet, the clipper was limited to the length of his electric cable which put a strain on backs and legs when the livelier sheep struggled to get free. The clipping takes three weeks, with Lena parcelling the piles of wool between cooking, feeding hens and ducks, and milking cows. And as the clipped sheep and their lambs are turned out again on to the sun-warmed hills, or down to a lowland farm for fattening up for market, the farm begins to hear new sounds, especially those of about ninety cows brought up from the parent farm to calve.

Not to be outdone is a Muscovy duck which somewhere in the depths of the hay dens in a barn has hatched out fifteen twittering, fluffy, lemon-and-brown ducklings. She parades them endlessly, competing for favours with the mothers of the newly born calves who shuffle uneasily and bellow warnings when human beings are near. Ray makes frequent circuits of the cows with his favourite dog Jed, now near-blind and deaf but needing few signals to tell him what to do—and keeping his distance from the cows and from the huge bulk of a Hereford bull which allows Ray to scratch its noble neck but never takes its eyes off Jed. Cows have been known to savage dogs who approach too close to their soft-featured offspring.

The same protective spirit lies in the ewes who will never allow a dog to approach too near their lambs, even being ready to attack the dog. The goats and their offspring at the farm are luckier, being guarded over by a fussy billy goat; no one watches over two fat and furry month-old pups who squirm along the floor of a stable. They all form a counter-balance to perhaps the worst time of year for the shepherd—the weaning of the lambs from their mothers. For about a fortnight, upwards of a thousand lambs, brought down to the farmhouse area, cry for their mothers, the air being rent day and night with their pitiable noises. Some mothers make the two-mile journey down from the fells in an attempt to reach and suckle their young, but when and if they meet again the lambs no longer search for their mothers' teats. Most of them are now taken down to the lowland farm to fatten for sale, while on the fells the main stock of ewes and replacement stock are sorted out in preparation for the next breeding season.

Before that comes round, however, there are two more important phases to come in the hill shepherd's year: dipping and the annual sales when a farmer's success is measured in the market. Dipping is a twice-yearly affair, the main one now being in late August or early September. By now autumn's fogs are beginning to creep in, hampering the last ritual of gathering for Ray. Sometimes deep fogs stretch the gather over three weeks, instead of the normal five days. One day Ian made a circuit of Swinhope Head and did not see a single sheep. Ray, on the other side of the fell, covered about 1,500 acres in sunshine. 'I felt on top of the world.'

The flock look remarkably fit after their earlier sufferings and they give Ray and Ian a rare old time in the sheep-dip trench, struggling to avoid the compulsory session—obligatory by law for a certain spell of time. Dipping is designed to give

protection from scab and other vermin, but it also acts as a
tonic, stimulating the sheep's skin and encouraging the growth
of wool. The 4ft 6in-deep dipping trench is alongside the
farmhouse, or 'in bye' as the shepherds call it, contrasting with
the 'out bye' of the open range.

Like dogs faced by a bath, sheep have no love of being
dipped. First-time lambs try to escape by climbing out from
the entry point. Those who have been through before take a
flying leap for the other end, remembering that that is the
way out; they always fall short and by the force of the leap
help Ray to complete their total immersion. Older rams,
worldly-wise and 200lb-plus in weight, with aggressive, curly
horns, fight to avoid the plunge into the murky 300 gallons.
Once in, leaving Ian sweating on the edge, they stretch out
their legs against the side walls to try to escape the indignity
of total dunking under the weight of Ray's long probe. They
always lose, but Ray is glad to join Ian in a breather before
the next one. Dipping provides frequent examples of the
prodigious knowledge that Ray and Ian share of their flock.
Ray points out twin rams, now two years old, with splendid
horns curving well out and away from the head, who had
been born of the farm's oldest ewe, thirteen years of age.

'That one there's a good 'un,' says Ray, pointing to a quiet
ewe with red marks on her ears. 'Apart from lambing and
dipping we hardly see her—she goes off on someone else's
land.' This was an example of the instinct, known as hefting,
by which a flock of sheep and their descendants tend to stay
on a certain area of land, known as a heft. Shepherds are used
to having sheep from other flocks among their stock and there
are general exchanges after certain gathers.

There was some doubt about the wisdom of the law com-
pelling a dip, which was now in its second year. Not that the
worth of the dip was questioned, rather the timing. The farm
had to advise when the dip was to take place, but there was a
feeling that the recommended timing was more related to the
problems of lowland, rather than hill, shepherding. The dip

was agreed to be essential because there had been signs that some shepherds had been lax. One result was that scab had come back into the country, something that Ray had never seen. Scab came to life in the flock when the cold weather began, starting in the roots of the wool, which the sheep then scratched, causing watery scabs which then multiplied. Dipping was vital to keep faith with the sheep industry as a whole.

The last batch to be dipped are the tup lambs, those who may live on to perpetuate the breed. First, however, comes the branding of their horns with a large S (for Swinhope) and a number, details which then go through into the farm's records. Branding, by hot iron, releases a sickening smell of scorched horn and puts Ray and Ian at severe risk of burning themselves as they struggle to hold the lively animals between their legs. This is almost the last chance for Ray to cast a critical eye over his stock for breeding purposes. One fine-looking lamb was singled out as not fit for breeding because there were too many grey hairs among the black around his eyes. 'Not very obvious yet—but the potential is there. Give it another year and more will show through.'

After the dipping and branding, Ray had talked with the farm's owners and decided which of the stock would be put into the Swaledale Association sales in the autumn; these would be registered with the Association. In the late summer each member shepherd or farmer is sent by the Association to check another member's sale stock. Each at some time may question a judgement that discards one of his borderline cases, but all accept that such judgements are in the long-term interests of the breed. Such risks as the over-development of the Roman-nosed face to the point where the lower lip is weakened, to the obvious detriment of the breed, must be guarded against.

With the breeding cycle complete the flock now falls into clearly defined categories, with their own hill-sheep labels. A tup lamb is a male lamb up to the first winter; a gimmer lamb is a female of the same term; wether lambs are castrated

males up to the first winter; male and female lambs during the first winter are called tup hogs and gimmer hogs respectively; after their first shearing sheep are known as one-, two-, three-year shearlings, and so on. And although to the casual eye sheep all look alike, the shepherd knows each one at a glance and its relationships with others in the flock: 'That one over there is from the same mother as that one there, but different fathers, and this one is uncle to the one by the gate—and they are the same age. These two are half-sisters, by the same father but from different ewes.'

Winter may still be some time off, but the Dents are making preparations, stowing hay on the fells, buying five tons of coal for the farmhouse, ordering ten stones of flour, and checking on the stocks in the deep-freeze. Before that come

the peak commercial and social events of the season, the sales.

The Swaledale Association organises a number of sales for ewes and rams, the most important to the Dents being the annual prize shows and sale of shearing rams at St John's Chapel, a modest village of plain-fronted cottages on the main road from Penrith to Bishop Auckland. For one long day the rural life there becomes aggressively urban and commercial.

The day began early for Ray and his son. They and the seventeen rams they had for sale were down in the village at 7.30am, when the light was crystal following overnight frost. Four of their rams were among the fifty being shown by large breeders, farmers with more than a hundred breeding ewes. Another dozen farmers sought the prize for small breeders.

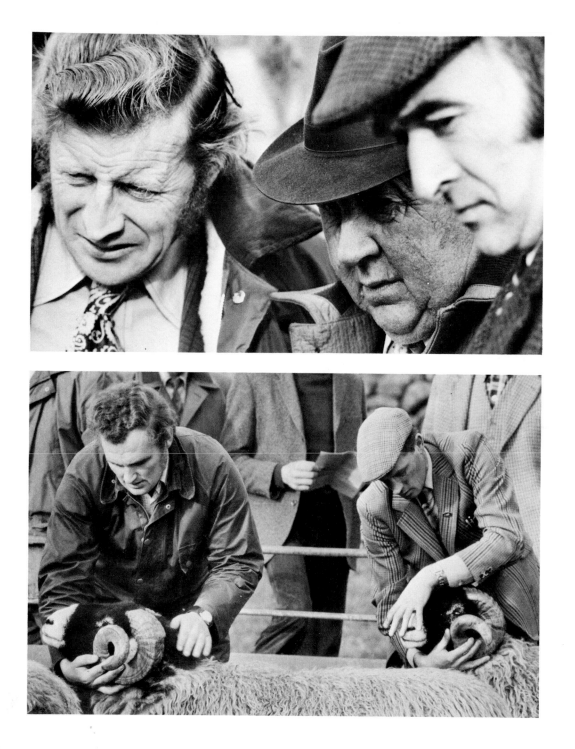

the four away to their quarters among the dozens of railed-off pens around the sale ring and left the show to others, for there would be much more judging before the winners were known.

Back at the show the small-breeders' champion was soon named and his shepherd wiped sweat from his forehead that owed nothing to the pale sun. There was no relief for the large breeders, where judging went on long after the clock on the square grey church had rung 10.30am, the twenty finalists

All the judging took place in a large field alongside the rudimentary, corrugated-iron sale-room, and by 8.30am the competing rams had been lined up, rear-on to the four judges, with the shepherds anxiously fussing over them like mothers at a baby show. The shepherds indeed looked nervous, frequently fluffing up the sheep wool, coloured a pale sherry by peat, to create a full-looking pelt. In contrast the back was smoothed, while facial hair and legs were cleaned and the division of black and white emphasised. The shepherds' faces, ruddy to a man under checked cap, trilby, or deerstalker, came to a pitch of anxiety as the judges, all fellow-shepherds, approached. Non-judges looked on critically, one offering the comment to a friend: 'That 'un's got fine legs'—and there wasn't a woman in sight.

Ray was disappointed but not unduly put out when his four rams failed to survive the preliminary weeding-out. The sale ring was more important than the show ring, after all, though he had expected a better showing for one of his rams. He led

being endlessly paraded until selection was narrowed to two rams. Even then another judge had to join in to settle the winner. It and the small-breeders' champion were then re-paraded, prodded, and pampered to settle the supreme championship.

This one did not take so long, the award going to the owner of the small-breeders' champion, Mrs Dorothy Wearmouth. It was her second success, the other being in 1973 when, as Dorothy Bell, she had been named as the first national Shepherd of the Year. She and her husband now had a long wait to learn how much the victory would be worth in the sale ring. In the meantime they had two trophies and £9.20 in prize money for their 10p entry fee.

Around the tall, cool bulk of the sale-ring building, interest was quickening. Each pen had its stock to be critically examined and pedigree sought. Much money was at stake. Legs hooked on the pen rails, hands leaning on shepherd crooks, the farmers endlessly talked sheep, within their banter and friendliness trying to search for a bargain ram or one that had the breeding potential that they were seeking. Owners, meanwhile, tried to encourage buyers, using local knowledge to try to assess what a shepherd was seeking. Activity around the pens only slightly diminished when the auctioneer mounted his podium overlooking the 20ft diameter ring inside the building.

With 471 rams to be sold in the day, Malcolm Peart was anxious to make a brisk start. His sing-song voice quickly concentrated commercial minds as the first ram was led into the sawdusted ring around which sat the shepherds in serried ranks of planked seating.

'Stand on, stand on. Here's a very good breeder. Who'll start me at a hundred? Who'll give me fifty, then? And at sixty, seventy, eighty, hundred . . .' His head swung from bidder to bidder, seeking out from the bunched benches the lowering of a head, flicker of an eyelid, faint raising of a programme, twitch of thumb on crook, or just the significant look, that signalled a bid.

'The bid's with you, sir, at 350. I'll take another ten—and who'll give me 400? Look at his fine wool—in the top twenty at the show. Your bid's in the ring at 450, sir, 450, 450, 450. Who'll give me another ten? 450, 450'—and with a brisk tap of his baton—'sold to John Doe there for £450. Next, please! Now, gentlemen, stand on, stand on. Here's another fine breeder—did well in the show . . .'

As one ram left the ring so another came in to be kept moving around the ring to allow the audience a last chance to confirm all that they had sensed during the prodding and feeling and inquiring in the pens outside.

Ray bid up to £185 for one ram, but demurred at £190; another that he bid up to £100 finally went for £300. One ram leapt out of the bidding ring into a small pen alongside the auctioneer just as the bidding began, was rescued by his owner, leapt over again, then twice rammed his head vigorously against the podium—all within the minute that it took Mr Peart, his face creased in laughter, to sell such a spirited animal for £640. Another owner refused to sell when his ram reached only £100. 'I prefer him to the money.' Some sales began painfully slowly at £50, then galloped into the hundreds, to be followed by another ram that to the untrained eye looked little different yet sold quickly for a knockdown £22.

Lunchtime came and knots of farmers left the ring to stroll past the ranks of green Land Rovers for lunch at the nearest pub, the Golden Lion, which had the auctioneer's voice piped through to keep customers in touch with the bidding. Others walked on to the King's Arms and the King's Head, opposite the Great War Memorial. On the way they passed a chemist's window, in which soap, shaving cream and Polaroid spectacles vied with tapeworm drench, veterinary iodine solution, sheep balsam, bonemeal and green castrating salve.

Back in the ring Norman Little had taken over from Malcom Peart, and the pace mounted as the sun sank. Ray's boss, John Vicker, tall and well booted, with a budding rose in his lapel, paid the highest price so far, £1,100, for Hartley Whelt. 'A lovely little animal, full of potential,' said Ray. 'There's no black in his wool (that is, among the facial white hair) and he's near enough what we're looking for. But you never know how good they are until you've sold their first draft ewes in five years' time.'

It would not be the costliest ram at Glen Whelt, where their supreme ram had cost them £2,900, while the record for a Swaledale had been £4,400, but it was the start of a quickening of price levels. In an attempt to make the sale as fair as possible the Association assembles a programme, then splits it at the half-way point. A ballot then decides which half will go first. The reasoning is historic. If an animal is good enough it will invariably bring a good price, but by the nature of the

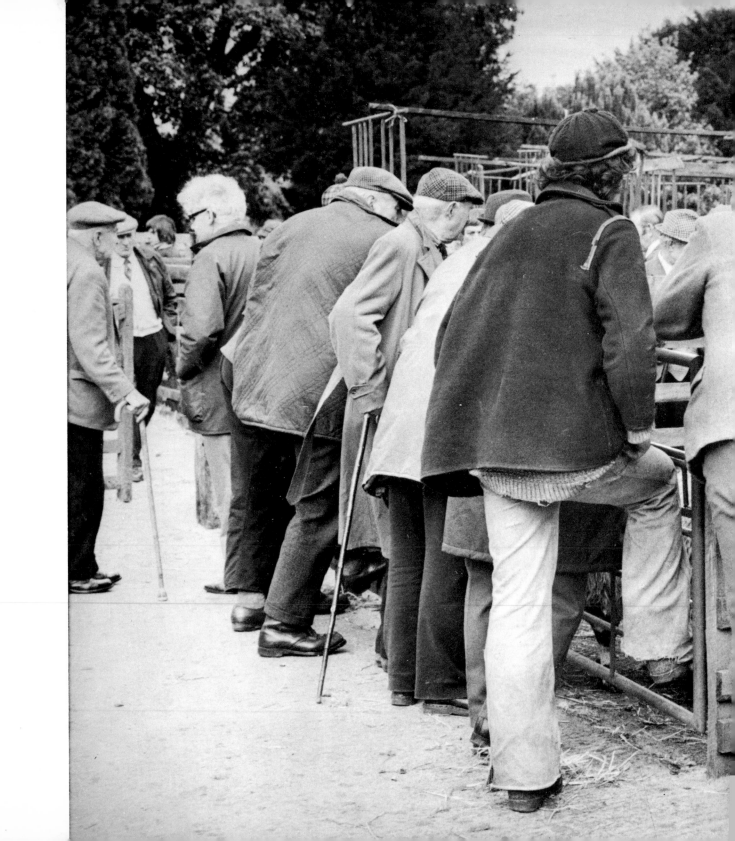

sale day the early hours are the quietest, while people are still assessing and still have the show ring to talk about. Some of the liveliest bidding can come in the late evening when shepherds and farmers begin to realise that they are risking going home without the rams that are essential to the coming breeding cycles. So Ray had not been too put out when his section was balloted to be sold in the later part of the day.

The sun had already lowered over Burnhope Moor by the time that the Glen Whelt rams came into the ring. The previous week their draft ewes (that is, those not required at the farm) had made a 'quite good' average of £41.60 at the Tow Law sale. Sadly, a wet year was to finish bleakly for the farm. The rams' average of £131 was about £90 down on the previous year and Ray's top hope, a splendidly aggressive fellow, made only £360. In contrast, the supreme show champion went at the day's end for a sale record of £2,400,

while another ram fetched £2,000.

Ray was naturally disappointed, but understood why it had not been such a productive year, aside from the weather. 'A number of the big farmers were down this year. It goes in cycles. Last year we had a good do and sold lots of tups to big buyers. But they don't want our tups again for some time because of the risk of getting too close inbreeding.'

He and his family had little chance to muse over what might have been. Back at the farm a group of ewes had been prepared for mating with a blue-faced Leicester ram to signal the start of a new breeding season; Lena was well stocked with winter provisions, and the hay was out on the fells. For Ian there was a chance of more square-dancing and perhaps a week away, while Ray, grown wise with the years to nature's cycle, shrugged his shoulders and brought out his easel and paints. Another year began to be born.